THE MOTORCYCLE TEST MANUAL

THE MOTORCYCLE TEST MANUAL

a complete guide to the new Compulsory Basic Training course

Gordon Cole

KOGAN
PAGE

Kogan Page Limited
120 Pentonville Road
London N1 9JN

in association with

Castrol UK Ltd
Burmah House
Pipers Way
Swindon SN3 1RE

© Gordon Cole 1991

British Library Cataloguing in Publication Data
A CIP record for this book is available from the
British Library.

ISBN 0 7494 0116 8

Typeset by DP Photosetting, Aylesbury, Bucks

Printed and bound in Great Britain by
Clays Ltd, St. Ives PLC

CONTENTS

For further information on the Castrol Motorcycle Product Range please contact:

Consumer Relations
Castrol (UK) Limited
Burmah Castrol House
Pipers Way
Swindon
Wiltshire SN3 1RE
Tel: 0793 512712

PREFACE

This book succeeds the former version of *The Castrol Motorcycle Test Manual – How To Pass Parts 1 and 2* by Gordon Cole, published in 1985.

Learning to drive any motorised vehicle is a gradual and continuous process. Contrary to the belief of many novice motorcyclists, a high standard of riding cannot possibly be achieved overnight, in a day or even a month. It takes years to achieve the required knowledge and skill to ride a motorcycle safely. Even then, there are some who never reach a high standard of riding, for various reasons.

Some novice motorcyclists think, wrongly, that all the experience and knowledge necessary to ride a motorcycle correctly can be gained by attending a motorcycle training scheme – it *cannot*. It has to be earned by applying over time what has been learned at the training scheme. With practice and self-discipline, the knowledge gained must be applied every time a motorcycle, scooter or moped is ridden.

The Department of Transport (DTp) Compulsory Basic Training (CBT) course has been devised to give you an excellent start, both in theory and practice. It will not only help you to pass the motorcycle test but will assist you in enjoying many years of skilled and accident-free riding. When you successfully complete the training course, remember what you were taught and apply this information every time you ride your machine. In doing so, you will make a contribution to your own safety and to that of others.

This book will show and explain the content of the new Compulsory Basic Training course and the motorcycle test, plus defensive riding techniques which are all-important when using our overcrowded and hazardous roads.

ACKNOWLEDGEMENTS

I would like to thank my friends Rick Lockyer, Graham Bartlett and the BMF-affiliated motorcycle instructors at the Harrow Driving Centre (Tel: 081-422 5883), which is an Approved Training Body.

I would also like to thank the following:

The British Standards Institute for giving permission to reproduce extracts from the British Standards (complete copies of which can be obtained from BSI Sales, Linford Wood, Milton Keynes, MK14 6LE);
The Driving Standards Agency for giving permission to reproduce forms DL26 and DL196;
Her Majesty's Stationary Office for giving permission to reproduce a UK driving licence (EC model) and the DVLA for supplying it;
Everitt W Vero & Co Ltd, 31–35 East Dulwich Road, London SE22 9AW (Tel: 081-693 6121), who supplied the safety helmets;
Bob Heath Visors, 6 Birmingham Road, Walsall WS1 2NA (Tel: 0922 611783), for supplying the visors;
and finally HGB Motorcycles, 67–71 Parkway, Ruislip Manor, Middlesex HA4 8NS (Tel: 0895 676451), for supplying the motorcycles.

INTRODUCTION

Statistics suggest that the type of people who use our roads and cause accidents – creating needless expense – and danger to others, display the 'I know it all, and don't need any training' attitude. This applies particularly to 16-year-olds who ride mopeds, and to the 20–24 age group who ride motorcycles. These two groups have more road accidents compared with other age groups who ride the same type of machine.

To combat the increasing number of road accidents, numerous governments have updated and introduced new legislation for the road user, in the interests of road safety. For example, in March 1982, a new two-part motorcycle test was introduced. In the same year, a two-year limit on a provisional licence for Group D was implemented as from 1 October.

The two-part test was devised by the Department of Transport to encourage novice motorcyclists to attend a beginners' training course with an authorised training organisation. The idea of the course was for the novice rider to attend and complete at least six hours of training. At the end of the course the student was issued with a certificate of attendance, whereby a part one test could be applied for and taken at an authorised training centre. Regardless of the standard of competence the student had reached at the end of the course, a certificate of attendance was issued. This in itself was potentially dangerous and, therefore, a new system has been introduced, with a phasing-out period for the old system.

Within the old legislation, the novice rider had the option to refuse any training, and apply directly to the Department of Transport for a part one test. The test was taken at one of the Heavy Goods Vehicle Driving Test Centres. This option was a loophole in the law, and proved a popular and cheap method of getting half way to obtaining a Group D licence, which made a mockery of the idea and purpose of the legislation for a two-part test.

The Compulsory Basic Training course, introduced on 1 December 1990, has no loopholes and has been devised to prevent certificates of training being issued after a certain number of hours tuition. Instead, certificates will have to be earned. Trainees will only be able to progress from one module of the course to the next when their training instructors are satisfied that they are ready to do so. A certificate of completion of training will only be issued when training instructors are satisfied that a trainee is sufficiently proficient to ride on his or her own. Should the trainee not reach the required standard of competence, he or she will have to receive further training until the required standard is reached. In the meantime, the trainee will not be allowed to ride a machine on the road.

This new system of training is designed primarily to improve the standard of road safety, especially among the higher risk age groups mentioned above. It was also introduced to bring the UK into line with European Community guidelines and regulations.

The motorcycle is one of the most economical forms of

transport, and since its invention it has given pleasure to millions. Over 387,000 Group D provisional licences have been issued to men and 184,000 to women. The number of people who have a full Group D licence is over 219,000 for men and over 22,000 for women. Because motorcyclists are open to the elements, particular caution is *always* needed when riding. If this caution is not exercised, accidents inevitably could occur.

To give an insight into the cost generated by road accidents in the United Kingdom, the following figures have been supplied by the Department of Transport. The total cost of road accidents in 1987 was estimated to be £4,990 million (£4,890 million in 1986). £3,990 million of the total cost in 1987 was attributable to 'personal injury' accidents, the remainder being accounted for by 'damage only' accidents. Of the total of personal injury accidents, 55 per cent occurred in built-up areas, 41 per cent in non-built-up areas, and five per cent on motorways.

What a waste of government money the cost of road accidents represents! If all road users (including pedestrians) were to concentrate, anticipate and be more patient, the accident rate could be drastically reduced and money could be saved and used instead to benefit the community.

Professional training is essential in any occupation if a high standard of competence is to be reached, and continuous use of the knowledge gained helps to achieve the best results at all times. The Compulsory Basic Training course is the start of your motorcycle career – never forget what you learn from it!

This book is divided into two parts. The first part covers, in detail, each element of the Compulsory Basic Training, taking you through each module, step-by-step. The second looks at every aspect of the test, and shows you what to do – and what not to do – on the day.

COMPULSORY BASIC TRAINING

MODULE ONE
THE BASICS

1

Aims of the course

Clothing and equipment

Speed

Documentation

Eyesight test

The Highway Code

Aims of the course

The Compulsory Basic Training (CBT) course for motorcyclists has been devised to ensure that learner motorcyclists and moped riders will not be able to ride on the road until the basic training course has been completed, and that instructors are satisfied that the rider is a safe one.

The training course will include both off-road and on-road assessment. The off-road element will cover: machine familiarisation; balance; controlled braking; rear observation; left and right-hand turns; figure-of-eight manoeuvre; slow riding and emergency braking. The on-road element will require trainees to put into practice the training already given and to display a sufficient degree of proficiency to be allowed to ride on the road on their own.

As from 1 December 1990, Compulsory Basic Training applies to every new rider of mopeds and motorcycles, ie those whose provisional licences are issued on or after 1 December 1990. They will not be permitted to ride on any public road (including riding to a training site), until they have satisfactorily completed Compulsory Basic Training, or are being accompanied while undergoing module four of the training course, under the supervision of an approved motorcycle instructor.

This will apply throughout Great Britain, including the Isle of Wight, the islands of Lewis and Harris, North Uist, Benbecula and South Uist, mainland Orkney, mainland Shetland, Skye and all islands (such as Anglesey) that are joined to the mainland by road. Residents of all other islands will be exempted from the requirement of Compulsory Basic Training, but only while riding on an exempted island.

Compulsory Basic Training will be available from Appointed Training Bodies (ATBs) authorised to provide it. In order to be authorised, ATBs have to employ instructors who have passed the Department of Transport's course on training and assessment techniques, and to operate sites approved by the Department of Transport for the off-road element of the course. Details of the location of Appointed Training Bodies can be acquired from motorcycle shops, the Road Safety Officer at your Civic Centre and from the police.

Once compulsory training has been satisfactorily completed, the instructor will issue a certificate which will validate a provisional licence, thereby allowing the holder to ride on the public highway. It must be borne in mind that a rider will still be limited to machines up to 125cc and up to 9KW power output. L-plates must still be displayed, and the rider will not be permitted to carry a pillion passenger on a solo machine.

The part one test will continue to operate until the end of May 1991, to allow existing riders to 'move out' of the old system. The length of the validity of a provisional motorcycle licence (Group A) is two years from the date of issue.

If the accompanied motorcycle test has not been taken and passed within the duration of the licence, the rider will be banned from riding for one year. The provisional licence has a two-year lifespan but is under constant review, and therefore, may be changed from two years to one year. You are thus advised to take and pass the accompanied motorcycle test well before the expiry date of the licence.

After passing the accompanied test, there is no restriction on engine size at present, but it is possible that a restriction could be applied following the harmonisation of EC rules after 1992. Car drivers with a provisional motorcycle entitlement will also have to obtain Compulsory Basic Training (CBT) validation with effect from 1 December 1990, if their car licence is issued on or after that date.

A certificate confirming the successful completion of the Compulsory Basic Training course will be supplied to approved training centres. There will be a nominal charge of just over £2.00 to each successful trainee for the certificate, although this fee may be included in the overall cost of the training. The cost of taking the Compulsory Basic Training course is up to the individual Appointed Training Body. You should, therefore, make enquiries at your local authorised training centre.

When you purchase a machine from a motorcycle shop, it will be delivered to your nearest Department of Transport Appointed Training Body. Should you purchase a machine privately, it will have to be delivered or ridden to the training site by a person who is a qualified rider, in order to comply with the law. Do *not* be tempted to ride the machine on the public highway before you are qualified to do so.

The primary object of module one of the Compulsory Basic Training (CBT) course is to make trainees aware of the aims of the course as a whole (ie to improve road safety and reduce the number of motorcycle accidents). This involves ensuring that all trainees fully understand the safety and legal requirements for riding a motorcycle on the public highway.

Clothing and equipment

Conspicuity

It is of the utmost importance that a motorcyclist is made as conspicuous as possible to other road users. The instructor is showing his trainees an orange-coloured tabard that provides fluorescent daytime brightness; this, combined with a 'Sam Brown' belt that gives retro-reflective brilliance is ideal for making yourself seen on the road. The headlamp should also be used at all times. It must be borne in mind that a motorcyclist is vulnerable every time the machine is ridden on the highway. Therefore, *be seen at all times*.

Clothing

Whenever you ride a motorcycle, scooter or moped, you should wear suitable clothing for comfort and safety. You must wear a safety helmet of approved design and standard, which must be fastened securely when worn. In adverse weather conditions, you should wear good waterproof clothing. There are many types available, some showerproof and some stormproof. It depends on how much you are prepared to pay, whether you keep warm and dry, or get cold and wet! Whatever you pay for your clothing, buy a light-coloured jacket. A fluorescent belt or tabard, as previously mentioned, are essential.

Always wear gloves when you ride your machine, so that your hands do not get cold and lose their sensitivity, which could be dangerous in an emergency. Good quality leather gloves will also give your hands protection if you should ever come off your machine. Never ride in training shoes, as they provide no protection at all, either in bad weather or in an accident. Always wear good, strong waterproof boots for the maximum degree of protection.

Correct clothing for a motorcyclist is of the utmost importance, not only for comfort, but safety too. The items of clothing required will be explained during the training course.

Compared to car drivers, motorcyclists are extremely vulnerable. They only have two wheels on which to balance instead of four, making them less stable; they have no solid protection surrounding them; their vehicles are smaller and much less visible and

depending on the machine size, it is difficult for them to accelerate out of potentially dangerous situations. This is especially true of smaller machines with less power.

Consequently, good-quality, conspicuous, protective clothing and equipment is not only important for comfort and safety, it could save *your* life.

Judging by the machine that is being ridden here, the rider must be an enthusiast, but not as far as his own safety is concerned. Note what is being worn, then consider what effect the road surface could have on the rider's hands, arms and body should he come off the machine. Make sure *you* wear the correct clothing.

Helmets

Students are being instructed here on how a safety helmet must be maintained, and the effect misuse can have on it. This, combined with eye protection, and the need to keep a visor or goggles clean and free from scratches so that vision is not impaired, are of vital importance.

The protection given by a helmet depends on the circumstances of the accident, and wearing a helmet cannot always prevent death or long-term disability.

A proportion of the energy of an impact is absorbed by the helmet, thereby reducing the force of the blow sustained by the head. The structure of the helmet may be damaged in absorbing this energy and any helmet that sustains a severe blow needs to be replaced, even if damage is not apparent.

To achieve the performance of which it is capable and to ensure stability on the head, a helmet should be as closely fitting as possible consistent with comfort; in use, it is essential that the helmet is securely fastened, with any chin strap under tension at all times.

The majority of trainee motorcyclists who arrive at a training centre for the first time do not wear suitable clothing required to ride a motorcycle, either for comfort or protection.

The first item of clothing a motorcyclist, moped or scooter rider must have is a Safety Helmet, as it is illegal to ride any two-wheeled motorised vehicle without one, except for the Sikh population. From 1 April 1989 all motorcycle helmets sold must be approved and Kitemarked to British Standard 6658. Helmets manufactured to BS6658 provide better protection against impacts, including those on the face bar of full face helmets, and are less likely to come off in an accident. Helmets approved to earlier British Standards are not illegal and can continue to be worn.

There are various styles of helmets, some offer more protection than others. The full-face type of helmet will give good all round protection. This style of helmet is more favourable than the open-face style of helmet. A visor is used for eye protection on a full-face helmet compared with goggles on an open style helmet.

If the shell of a helmet is made of a thermoplastics material or of a material which is known to be adversely affected by contact with hydrocarbons, cleaning fluids, paints, transfers or other extraneous additions, then the helmet shall carry on its information label an appropriate warning.

The definitions that apply to a safety helmet are numerous. The following definitions apply to BS6658.

Helmet Headwear primarily intended to protect against a blow to the part of the wearer's head that lies above the basic plane, without preventing adequate peripheral vision.

Shell The hard, smooth material that provides the general outer form of the helmet.

Protective Padding Liner material provided to absorb impact energy.

Comfort Padding Soft material provided to ensure a close fit to the wearer.

Retention System The complete assembly that prevents the helmet coming off the head.

Quick-Release Mechanism A system attached to, or incorporated in, the helmet that allows the retention system to be fastened and unfastened quickly.

Chin Strap A strap that passes under the wearer's chin or lower jaw and is intended to retain the helmet on the head under impact.

Chin Cup A device that fits around the point of the wearer's chin, and must have a secondary strap which is required by Law.

Chin Guard An extension of the shell covering the lower part of the face.

Face Cover An accessory protecting the lower part of the face against mud, stones and weather.

Peak A semi-rigid extension of the shell above the eyes.

Visor, Eye Screen A transparent protective screen extending over the eyes and covering part or all of the face.

Goggles Eye-protectors having a one piece protective lens or individual lenses designed to cover the orbital cavities and to be in contact with the face around the eyes.

Basic Plane:
(1) Of a human head. A plane at the level of the external auditory meatus (external ear opening) and the inferior margin of the orbit (lower edge of the eye socket).
(2) Of a Headform. That plane relative to the helmet that corresponds to the basic plane of the head that the helmet is intended to fit.
(3) Of a Helmet. That plane relative to the helmet that corresponds to the basic plane of the head that the helmet is intended to fit.

Reference Plane A plane relative to a headform, parallel to the basic plane and at a distance above it specified in BS6489.

Central Vertical Axis The line relative to a human head or headform or helmet that lies in the plane of symmetry, and what is normal to the basic plane at a point equidistant from the front and back of the head or the headform or (for helmets) of the headform that simulates the head that the helmet is intended to fit.

Longitudinal Vertical Plane The vertical plane of symmetry of a human head or headform or of a helmet as it is intended to be worn on the head.

Central Transverse Vertical Plane A plane at right angles to the longitudinal vertical plane and passing through the central vertical axis.

Size of helmet The size of the head which the inner parts and retention system of the helmet are designed to fit.

NOTE: Several different sizes of helmet may be manufactured from one size of outer shell.

Eye Protection A helmet intended for use with goggles shall carry on its information label an appropriate warning. A helmet not intended for use with goggles shall be fitted with a visor or with means for fitting one and shall carry on its information label an appropriate warning.

Where a helmet is fitted or supplied by the manufacturer with a visor, the visor shall not be tinted and shall comply with BS4110. Opening of the visor shall not cause abrasion of the visor within the field of peripheral vision complying with BS6489.

Warning Label Every helmet having a shell made of thermoplastics material shall bear a warning label, attached to the chin strap or to a suitable stud, bearing the words BSI Warning DO NOT PAINT OR APPLY SOLVENTS.

This brief summary of British Standard Specifications for protective helmets for Vehicle Users is for general guidance. Should a full specification of BS6658 be required, please contact the British Standards Institute.*

* Many thanks to the British Standards Institute for their kind permission to reproduce the above material in this book.

A student arrived at a test centre with this helmet which has the protective padding missing from the front section, rendering this part of the helmet useless in a time of need. It is advisable not to purchase a second-hand helmet, not even from a friend, regardless of its condition.

Here, the helmet has been placed on the saddle. This may seem a safe place to put it, but should a gust of wind or a careless hand knock it to the ground, it could render the helmet useless. For the same reason, never hang your helmet from the mirror or the handlebars.

The requirement to wear a helmet does not apply if you are a follower of the Sikh religion and wear a turban.

Visors

It is illegal for drivers or pillion passengers (not in a side car) to use eye protection (ie visor, goggles, etc.) while riding a motorcycle that does not conform to safety standards.

One of the following three codes must be marked on the eye-protector lens:

BS4110**XA**   BS4110**YA**   BS4110**ZA**

A 6.5mm steel ball is used to test the impact resistance of eye-protectors and there are three impact speeds in BS4110: X, Y and Z. These are measured in metres per second (mps).

XA = 12 mps = 27 mph = LOW protection from small flying objects. This low impact test is for glass protectors only.

YA = 45 mps = 101 mph = MEDIUM protection from small flying objects.

ZA = 70 mps = 154 mph = GOOD protection from small flying objects.

All 1mm and 1.5mm thick visors exceed the **ZA** 154 mph impact test. The 'A' means the eye-protector has passed the abrasion-resistance test to the BS4110 standard. 'A' standard visors will not abrade as easily as cheaper, uncoated visors and, therefore, they give longer lasting, safer vision. Tinted eye-protectors must also be marked *day time vision only*.

A smoked visor is legal in daylight, but should not be worn during premature darkness or darkness, or in adverse weather conditions.

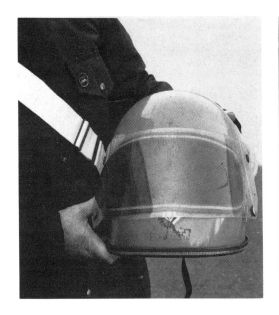

A student arrived at a training centre with this helmet which can only be classed as useless. The visor is so badly scratched that it impairs vision in daylight, and so it is illegal and dangerous during the hours of darkness. The reply the student gave when asked where he got the helmet was 'from a friend, but I got it cheap'. Some friend!

To help prevent steaming or misting up inside the visor, an anti-mist substance can be sprayed on to a clean duster and applied to the visor.

The inside of the visor is being wiped with a duster which has anti-mist substance on it. The substance is effective only for a limited time and, therefore, will have to be reapplied at frequent intervals. The anti-mist substance should not be sprayed directly on to a visor, but on to a duster as shown previously.

This instructor is wearing a piece of rubber on his glove called a Vee Wipe. The straight edge is used to wipe the exterior of the visor, therefore maintaining the best possible vision in adverse weather and in spray created by other road users.

Speed

During the introduction to the course, the need to drive at the correct speed according to road and traffic conditions will be firmly impressed upon all trainees. This aspect of riding is covered more fully later in the course and its absolute importance (in terms of your own safety and that of other road users) is strongly emphasised.

Speed at the wrong time and place has ended in disaster for the rider of this machine. It could have been a fatal accident due to poor machine control.

Documentation

The instructor here is checking all documentation to ensure that it meets all the legal requirements before the practical training starts. Documents which have to be shown are: insurance certificate; provisional driving licence; MOT certificate if the machine is three or more years old, and road fund tax disc, which should be fixed and displayed on the left hand side of the machine.

Should any document not comply with the law, the practical on-road riding part (module 4) of the course cannot be conducted.

Eyesight test

After the introductory talk on the aims and other aspects of the course, students will be required to read a number plate at the distance required by law.

The student (holding the helmet) is reading a number plate attached to the side of a building. It is of the utmost importance that you can read a vehicle registration plate containing letters and figures 79.4mm high at a distance of 20.5 metres (with the aid of glasses or contact lenses if worn). It is not permitted to put on a pair of glasses to read a number plate and then take them off.

The Highway Code

The Highway Code must be studied and its contents read and understood before attending a Compulsory Basic Training course.

MODULE TWO PRACTICAL ON-SITE TRAINING

2

The training centre

Your machine

Becoming familiar with the motorcycle

Basic machine checks

Using the stand

Wheeling the machine, proper balance and braking

Starting and stopping the engine

Riding the machine under control

Controlled braking using both brakes

Any questions?

The training centre

At one training centre there may be one instructor, at another there could be more. Here, three instructors are asking the trainees questions about the training that they have received previously (if any).

The ratio of instructor to trainees should be one instructor to four trainees for modules two and three and one instructor to two trainees for module four – practical on-road riding. The minimum size of the training site required for use by a maximum of two trainees and one instructor is 80 × 30 feet. The size of the site should increase in proportion to the number of trainees and instructors using the area.

Your machine

It does not matter what type or model of machine you ride, provided it complies with the law and with the legislation relating to learner riders.

Becoming familiar with the motorcycle

A thorough explanation of machine controls and switches is given to the trainees. The instructor will work systematically from one end of the machine to the other, and from side to side. After the controls lesson, the students must try to use all the controls while riding the machine. This should be achieved without having to look at the controls when using them.

While students are being shown the controls of a motorcycle, their function is also explained.

The kick-start pedal and method of starting the engine is explained.

The instructor explains where the foot should be placed on the foot rest, so that the gear lever can be used as and when required.

Make sure you understand and can operate all the controls before moving off.

Basic machine checks

Regardless of whether a machine is new or second hand, it will be inspected. Should a serious (or dangerous) fault be found, the student will not be allowed to ride the machine until the fault has been rectified.

These instructors have found a fault with the front wheel bearing of this machine. A student should contact the motorcycle dealer to have the fault corrected.

The trainee is answering questions on machine maintenance put to him by the instructor. It is very important that a trainee is aware of what and how to check and service various parts of a machine. Otherwise, it could become potentially dangerous, not only to the rider, but to other road users too.

All trainees should be shown, and should learn, how to: check that there is sufficient oil in the machine; correct chain tension and check its condition; adjust the front and rear brake cable correctly; check that the indicators, brakes, headlamp, rear lights and horn are all fully operational and clean; check the steering head play, suspension, wheels and tightness of all nuts and bolts and check the condition of the tyres and their correct pressures.

It is an obligatory requirement that each module of the training syllabus is satisfactorily completed before a trainee can proceed onto the next module. Each trainee's ability and level of competence will be recorded.

This trainee is being questioned on the function and maintenance of various controls.

Numerous questions on machine maintenance and other aspects of motorcycling will be put to the trainee during the course. The instructor is making notes on the answers given by the student. The answers must satisfy the instructor that the trainee is competent in the subject on which he is questioned.

Here, the instructor has asked the student how to check the chain tension, and if required, how to adjust it. The trainee is explaining why the chain must not be too loose or too tight, and how to adjust it.

Using the stand

Trainees are shown the correct way to put a motorcycle on the centre stand.

The trainees are shown the incorrect way of putting a machine on the centre stand, and an explanation is given of the problems and dangers that may arise if this is done.

Wheeling the machine, proper balance and braking

This trainee is wheeling his machine round to the right and then to the left, demonstrating to the instructor that proper balance is being maintained. He then brings the machine to a halt by proper use of the front brake. The purpose of this exercise is for trainees to feel and appreciate the weight of the machine before it is ridden.

Starting and stopping the engine

Make sure the fuel tap is turned to the 'on' position before starting the engine. Should you move off before doing so, a dangerous situation could arise, not only for you, but for other road users too. Also check that the neutral gear is selected and the ignition is switched on before trying to start the engine, as and when you are requested to do so.

The instructor has demonstrated how to start the engine by using the kick-start pedal, and then how to stop the engine by switching the ignition off. This training is given because not all machines have an electric engine starter or engine kill switch fitted. Trainees, therefore, are taught the basic principles of starting and stopping an engine. This student is learning how to do this. As the machine will not be ridden, the student is not wearing his helmet.

This rider is trying to start the engine while the machine is on the centre stand. The dangers of this procedure are not obvious to the trainee. He will be advised by an instructor.

This trainee has forgotten to raise the side stand before moving off. This mistake could be fatal if committed on the highway. Always make sure the side and or centre stand(s) are in the up position once you have mounted the machine, and *before* starting the engine.

The students are learning to start the engine by using the kick-start, regardless of whether a machine is fitted with a push-button electric starter. The proper use of other controls while the engine is running is the next important thing to be shown.

The instructor is showing the trainee the importance of correct riding position, so that all controls can be used. The clutch and brake levers should be operated with all four fingers.

The trainee is about to move off for the first time. The instructor is ready to assist should the need arise.

The student is learning how to use the clutch and move off without stalling the engine.

Riding the machine under control

This trainee is learning to ride in a straight line, and to bring the machine to a controlled stop by using either brake.

Controlled braking using both brakes

The trainee is learning to use the brakes and stop the machine without stalling the engine. The instructor gives the trainee instructions on how to achieve a controlled stop.

This instructor is demonstrating the adverse effect on machine control of improper use of the front brake. Note the rear wheel has locked, causing skidding and loss of control.

This instructor is demonstrating what happens to a motorcycle when only the front brake is used. Note how the weight of the machine is thrown forward. A full explanation of the proper use of brakes will be given during the training course.

The instructor is demonstrating the importance of using both brakes correctly to achieve a safe and controlled stop.

TOTAL STOPPING DISTANCE

Distance travelled assuming an about average reaction time

M.P.H	Reaction Distance	Braking Distance	Total Stopping Distance
	ft.	ft.	ft.
20	20	20	40
30	30	45	75
40	40	80	120
50	50	125	175
60	60	180	240
70	70	245	315

REMEMBER – These braking distances only apply on dry road surfaces. On wet roads, they could double.

When learning how to brake properly, it is extremely important that you are aware of the minimum stopping distances, especially in adverse weather conditions.

Any questions?

The instructor here is discussing riding techniques with the group of trainees who have been assigned to him. Please put any questions you would like answered to the instructors. They are there to *help* you.

MODULE THREE PRACTICAL ON-SITE RIDING

3

Riding in practice

Rear observation

Left and right-hand turns

The figure of eight

Slow and controlled riding

The emergency stop

Riding in practice

Having become thoroughly familiar with your machine, and satisfied your instructor that this is the case, you move onto module three where you learn and practise different riding manoeuvres and practical use of machine controls on the test centre site.

This student is taking good rear observation. A glance over the shoulder is *not* good enough, and could be dangerous.

The instructor is making sure the trainee takes rear observation once a manoeuvre has been completed, so that he is aware of any following traffic.

Rear observation

The vital importance of rear observation will be explained to you on numerous occasions during the training course. This trainee is taking good rear observation (known as the 'life saver') before turning right. Note how the head is turned while the rider maintains a steady course.

The instructor is explaining The System of Motorcycle Control (see page 113) for turning left. He will invite the class to ask questions as the lecture proceeds.

Students are having The System of Motorcycle Control explained to them and its importance on the approach to, and before, turning right.

Left and right-hand turns

These trainees are going through the basics of turning right by using the observation, signal, manoeuvre (OSM) and position, speed, look (PSL) routines.

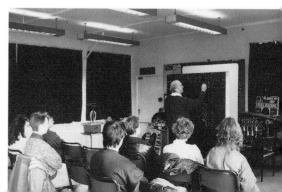

The instructor is explaining to students the route to be taken during riding practice.

This trainee is learning to take effective observation before emerging at a junction.

These students are practising right-hand turns. Note the correct rear observation being taken by the following rider and the correct position on the road of the leading rider.

The figure of eight

The trainee is being instructed on how to use the appropriate controls, so that the figure of eight can be accomplished. This requires good machine control and balance.

The trainee is maintaining control of his machine and achieving a good standard of balance.

This student has been using the brake and clutch levers incorrectly. Therefore, the instructor is explaining how they should be used.

The instructor is watching a trainee riding in a figure of eight. Correct machine control and balance should be achieved to reach a satisfactory standard of riding.

Group discussions are encouraged so that any points that trainees might have can be mentioned and, if need be, emphasised.

These trainees are putting into practice what they have been shown.

Slow and controlled riding

The instructor is demonstrating how and what controls should be used to ride slowly in a confined space.

A trainee has come off his machine while going through one of the numerous exercises, due to lack of machine control and balance.

The trainees are making good progress. Note the instructors are watching every move the trainees make. Should a fault be made, the student will know about it!

Balance and machine control is of absolute importance in order to ride slowly through confined and hazardous spaces, such as in heavy traffic.

This instructor is watching a trainee ride through a slalom of cones. Correct use of the brakes and other controls is essential for maintaining balance and control.

All trainees on a course will have their riding skills assessed at frequent intervals. This trainee is doing a slow riding exercise. The instructor is looking for proper use of the controls and balance.

The emergency stop

Instruction is given on the controlled, progressive use and distribution of braking required for different types of road surfaces. The instructor has raised an arm, this being the signal for the trainee to apply the brakes as in an emergency situation. Proper use of the brakes and control of the machine are of the utmost importance.

MODULE FOUR
PRACTICAL
ON-ROAD RIDING

4

The riding assessment

Riding defensively and anticipating other road users

The value of rear observation

Road position

Weather conditions and road surfaces

Intelligent use of speed

Traffic lights

The riding assessment

In the final objective of the training course, every trainee will have a riding assessment. The instructor follows the trainee and gives all directional instructions by using a one-way radio (as is done in the accompanied test itself).

The aim of the practical on-road riding module is to ride competently and safely in as great a variety of road traffic situations as possible.

This rider is looking well ahead and, in doing so, has seen a vehicle approaching from his right. By planning well ahead, the rider has allowed himself adequate time to react to the potential danger approaching. If you look late, an accident could occur.

Riding defensively and anticipating other road users

The driver of the car has crossed the path of the rider, and in doing so, has forced the rider to make an emergency stop to avoid a collision. An accident was avoided because the rider was concentrating and was, therefore, able to anticipate the action taken by the driver.

There have been numerous fatal rider/driver accidents at junctions. The reasons for these are many. The most common cause is a driver not making the required effort to look right, left and right again before emerging from a junction. The speed and distance of an approaching motorcyclist are frequently misjudged. A driver waiting at a junction sees a motorcyclist approaching, and his thought is often 'it's only a motorcyclist'. In consequence, the driver emerges into the path of the motorcyclist, hoping the rider will stop. He cannot, sometimes because the road is wet. The driver has caused another accident. Make sure your presence on the road is seen by other road users by applying what you learn during the training course.

By concentrating and looking well ahead, the rider is able to anticipate the car emerging into his path. He was, therefore, ready to adjust speed the moment the car started to do so. Lack of concentration and judgement by opposing road users has been the cause of many serious and fatal road accidents. Look and plan well ahead.

Many potential dangers can be seen on the approach to this crossroads. The road surface is covered with wet leaves, an oncoming bus is reducing the width of the road and a vehicle can be seen on the left, waiting to emerge into the junction.

Rear observation should be taken and speed reduced. Bearing in mind the dangerous road surface, stopping should be considered. This would allow the vehicles to proceed on their respective courses. Better to make slow progress than none at all!

On the approach to a junction where road works are present, a rider should anticipate a vehicle approaching from the road to be joined. If the intention is to turn right at the end of the road, the rider will have to pass the road works, then move back to the left of the hazard line. Failure to do so will put a rider in a potentially dangerous position.

As you approach this crossroads, your intention is to follow the road ahead. Buildings obscure your view to either side and, therefore, any traffic approaching the junction cannot be seen. Rear observation should be taken and speed reduced. Consider using the horn while looking right, left and right again.

The value of rear observation

Use rear observation at the appropriate times, especially when overtaking.

The rider is taking effective rear observation by looking over his left shoulder, making sure he is well clear of the vehicle that he has been overtaking before moving back to the left-hand side of the road.

The rider has to pass a stationary vehicle. Before a change of course is made the rider should make sure it is safe to do so and a signal of intent is given. Rear observation is being taken to check the position and speed of any following traffic before a signal is given, bearing in mind a signal gives you no right of way whatsoever.

Road position   *For normal driving*

This rider is in the correct position on the road for normal driving.

This rider has positioned the machine too far from the kerb for normal riding, and in doing so, has created a potentially dangerous situation for another road user and himself.

This rider is riding far too close to the kerb.

It is extremely important when riding to leave sufficient space between you and any vehicle you may be following.

This motorcyclist is following a car far too closely and is, therefore, well outside the bounds of safety. Both vehicles are travelling at 30 mph. Should the car suddenly stop before the driver has looked behind or even considered using the mirrors, a serious accident could occur. A rider should maintain a safe following distance (applying the two second rule which is covered on the course) from the vehicle in front, thereby allowing time and distance to act on any sudden action taken by the driver of that vehicle.

Weather conditions and road surfaces

Pay due regard to the effects of weather conditions, and be aware of the various types of road surfaces. The former can often drastically affect the latter.

Fallen leaves have created an ill-defined kerb line. Therefore, a wider course than normal should be taken when making a left turn, thus avoiding the kerb.

Stone setts (cobblestones) can still be encountered in many towns and cities. Extreme caution should be taken when riding on this type of surface. Loss of control can occur very easily, particularly when the surface is wet.

Deep ruts can adversely affect balance, steering and braking, even more so when the road surface is wet.

Loose stone chippings can also affect balance, steering and braking, so approach this kind of surface with caution.

Wet leaves on the road are dangerous to any road user, but especially to a motorcyclist approaching a junction. The System of Motorcycle Control must be applied in good time. In doing so, the junction is approached at a slow speed, thereby avoiding harsh use of the brakes at the last moment.

Intelligent use of speed

Even in this situation, when the road surface and weather conditions are good and the road ahead is clear, you must still comply with the speed limit, which, in this case, is 30 miles per hour.

Whatever the circumstances, you must use speed intelligently, safely and within the legal limit!

Traffic lights

You must always comply with traffic light signals. Red and amber lights together mean STOP and Green means you may PROCEED *if it is safe to do so*.

MODULE FIVE
CONCLUSION
AND VALIDATION

5

The end of the course

Issue of validation certificate

The need for further training

The end of the course

When you have completed the practical on-road ride and are back at the training site, the instructor will ask you to park your machine and remove your helmet and radio equipment.

The conclusion of the course will consist of a brief theory lesson, the content of which will cover:

(1) Knowing the effect of drink, fatigue, illness, drugs etc on riding behaviour.
(2) Knowing how to reduce the risk of an accident.
(3) Being aware that courtesy and consideration towards other road users is very important.

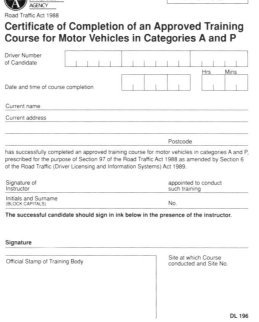

DSA DRIVING STANDARDS AGENCY

Road Traffic Act 1988

000001

Certificate of Completion of an Approved Training Course for Motor Vehicles in Categories A and P

Driver Number of Candidate

Date and time of course completion   Hrs   Mins

Current name

Current address

Postcode

has successfully completed an approved training course for motor vehicles in categories A and P, prescribed for the purpose of Section 97 of the Road Traffic Act 1988 as amended by Section 6 of the Road Traffic (Driver Licensing and Information Systems) Act 1989.

Signature of Instructor   appointed to conduct such training

Initials and Surname (BLOCK CAPITALS)   No.

The successful candidate should sign in ink below in the presence of the instructor.

Signature

Official Stamp of Training Body   Site at which Course conducted and Site No.

DL 196

An Executive Agency of the Department of Transport

Issue of validation certificate

When each module of the training course has been completed, the trainee's standard of competence for each element of the modules will be recorded on the instructor's report sheet. This will be the basis for deciding whether the trainee has completed his or her training to a satisfactory standard.

If it is judged that you have completed the Compulsory Basic Training course to a sufficiently safe and competent standard, you will be issued with a certificate stating that you have done so. This certificate (DL 196 as shown here) will validate your provisional licence and allow you to ride your machine on the public highway. However, until you pass your test, you are restricted to riding machines with the maximum engine size of 125cc only. You must also display L-plates at all times and you are prohibited from carrying a pillion passenger. The certificate must accompany your application for the on-road accompanied test.

The need for further training

Should you fail to complete the Compulsory Basic Training course satisfactorily, then you should discuss the reasons for this with your instructor. He will advise you as to the further training you will need before you can receive a certificate of validation and ride on the public highway.

Even if you have completed CBT successfully, your instructor will still advise you as to any further training you may need to pass your test.

If you need any further information on how to get started with your training, phone the Department of Transport's BIKELINE *free* on 0800 400 483.

THE TEST

THE MOTORCYCLE TEST

6

Applying for your test

Your provisional motorcycle licence is valid for two years from when it is issued. If you do not pass the motorcycle test before this licence expires, then you will be prohibited from riding on the public highway for one year. It is, therefore, advisable to apply for your test very soon after successfully completing the Compulsory Basic Training.

To apply for your motorcycle test, you must complete the appropriate form (shown here) and send it off with your CBT certificate of validation to the address given on the reverse of the notes attached to the form. The easiest place to pick up one of these forms is at your nearest main Post Office.

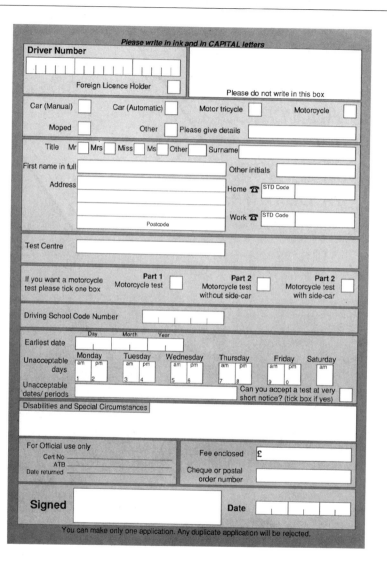

Having applied, paid for and had a date set for your test, you should arrive at your appointed test centre on the appointed day and (preferably) a few minutes before the time stated on your test appointment card which is sent to you in advance.

The candidate here is making a final adjustment to his helmet, so that he is able to hear the instructions given by the examiner. If any instructions given by the examiner are not understood for one reason or another, you should follow the procedure as explained to you by the examiner at the start of the test.

Before you begin

The eyesight test

The examiner asks the candidate to read a number plate on a particular vehicle. You will be required to read a number plate at a distance just over the minimum required by law. If you cannot read the plate, the examiner will take you a little nearer and ask you to read the same number plate again. If you still cannot read it, the examiner will ask you to go with him to the office to get a tape measure supplied by the Department of Transport. The exact distance will then be measured from the number plate to the point where you should be able to read it, ie 67ft for letters and figures $3\frac{1}{8}$ in. high on the numberplate or 75ft for letters and figures $3\frac{1}{2}$ in. high on the number plate.

If you cannot read the numberplate, you will be failed for not being able to comply with the requirements of the eyesight test.

If you wear glasses or contact lenses to read a number plate, you must continue to wear them for the rest of the test. Candidates who are dumb or who cannot read and write will be requested to draw the letters and numbers with pen and paper supplied by the examiner. Once you have read the number-plate, the examiner will ask you to start the engine of your machine.

One-way radio communication

Should you have any doubt as to what the examiner has explained to you before the test, ask him to repeat what he has said.

During the test, the examiner gives riding instructions to the candidate by means of one-way radio communication. You cannot, therefore, converse with him while you are riding.

Take proper precautions before starting the engine

Before you start the engine of your machine, make sure the fuel and ignition are switched to the *on* position, and the gear lever is in neutral. This rider is making sure that neutral gear is selected before attempting to start the engine.

Requirements of the test

Proper use of Accelerator, Clutch, Gears, Footbrake, Handbrake, Steering

Accelerator (Throttle)

The accelerator should be used with reasonable smoothness. Do not turn the throttle suddenly, especially when moving off. When accelerating, do so progressively as the situation demands and *do not* accelerate while another vehicle is overtaking you. It is also important that you close the throttle smoothly when slowing down.

Too much throttle at the wrong time and place is a fault that could be dangerous. A rider who has the expertise to use the throttle and other controls individually or in conjunction with each other correctly and at the right time and place, will have the machine under control at all times. A rider should plan well ahead and apply 'acceleration sense'. In doing so, he or she will be able to vary the speed of the machine to meet any changing road and traffic conditions that can be seen ahead. Always remember that a motorcycle should be ridden at a speed which ensures that the rider can always stop within the distance that he or she can see to be clear.

Clutch

The clutch must be used smoothly and correctly when moving off, changing gear and in conjunction with the brakes when stopping. You should be able to control and operate the clutch lever correctly and with reasonable smoothness. Do not suddenly release the lever, or coast with the lever in. This applies particularly after changing gear on the approach to a junction or hazard. Misuse of the clutch at any time could be dangerous.

Gears

The appropriate gear should be selected to suit the road and traffic conditions at the time, so that you are travelling at the correct speed with the correct gear engaged. You should plan your riding well ahead, so that you are aware of, and can anticipate, the actions of other road users and pedestrians. Do not race or labour an engine when a higher or lower gear should be used and do not look down at the controls when changing gear.

When approaching a junction or hazard, do not make a late or hurried change of gear, or change down to a lower gear too early. After changing gear do not coast. Plan your riding so that you give yourself time and distance to release the clutch lever, so that the gear selected is in use.

Do not select a gear which would be unsuitable for the prevailing conditions, eg approaching a sharp bend or corner in a high gear, when the road speed and conditions demand a lower gear. A lower gear would enable the rider to accelerate out of a hazard, if it is safe to, or to stop more easily if necessary.

Improper use of the gears at the wrong time or place could be dangerous.

Footbrake (rear brake)

Look well ahead and plan your riding. When you use the rear brake, do so smoothly and in good time. Do not brake late or hard. If you brake so late that you increase the danger which you are trying to avoid in stopping, or endanger the traffic behind you, you could create a potentially dangerous situation. Not using the rear brake in conjunction with the front brake, or using the front brake only when both brakes should be used, could also be dangerous.

Handbrake (front brake)

A vital aspect of riding a motorcycle is that a rider must recognise and respect the condition of the road surface and any obstacles on it. Should a rider not be aware of an adverse road surface and have to apply the brakes hard, a serious accident could occur.

To be able to stop at any speed on a good, dry road the front brake is the most effective. All round braking efficiency is increased by a much lighter use of the rear brake at the same time as the front, which will ensure that there is no risk of the rear wheel locking.

On the approach to a hazard, any reduction in road speed should be accomplished by proper use of the brakes or by deceleration (by closing the throttle) and *not* by changing to a lower gear.

Remember the rules of braking:

1 Brake only when the machine is straight and upright. Always brake in plenty of time.
2 Brake pressure should vary according to road surface conditions. Firm braking is needed on coarse, dry roads and gentle braking on loose or slippery surfaces.
3 On long, steep descents, brake firmly on the straight sections and rear brake only on the bends. Select a low gear at the start of the descent.
4 Avoid using the front brake when the machine is banked over, turning on wet, cambered surfaces, or where the surface is slippery, loose, greasy, icy, polished or leaf-covered.
5 On a good, dry road surface, braking should be 75% front brake and 25% rear. On a wet surface, the distribution of braking should be 50% front brake and 50% rear.

You should remember that your machine should always be in the correct place on the road, travelling at the correct speed for the prevailing road and traffic conditions and with the correct gear engaged to suit the speed of the engine and road speed of the machine.

Steering
It is important that you keep both hands on the handlebars at all times, unless you are giving an arm signal. Always steer a steady course. Do not wobble, even at slow speeds and do not wander from lane to lane. When passing a row of stationary vehicles, steer a steady and correct course past them. You must be aware that a car door could be opened or a pedestrian could step out. Do not weave in and out between parked vehicles.

When approaching and turning a corner, steer a steady course smoothly and not in jerky movements. Do not oversteer or understeer. Do not swing out before or after left or right-hand turns. It is of the utmost importance that you position your machine correctly during normal riding and before making any turn.

If you have to change course for any reason, take effective rear observation first to make sure it is safe to do so.

This rider is weaving about on the road which could be dangerous if any traffic were following or approaching. Always steer a steady course.

This rider has approached the junction too fast, and has, therefore, swung out wide while turning, creating the situation where a collision might occur.

This rider has turned too late at the junction. Consequently, he is doing a 'swan's neck' turn while trying to get back on course. This fault can be dangerous for other road users and pedestrians.

When turning left, keep well to the left if there is nothing to stop you from doing so. Do *not* swing out before turning left as this rider is doing.

It is potentially dangerous to weave in and out between stationary vehicles when a straight course could be taken. The examiner (the second rider) is steering the correct course. He will report the candidate for steering, position and observation faults.

Move away safely and under control

This rider is taking good rear observation before he moves away, by looking over his right shoulder.

The emergency stop

During the first part of the test, the examiner will give you the instruction, 'pull up on the left at a convenient place, please'. The purpose of this request is for the examiner to conduct the emergency stop exercise. The wording for this exercise is, 'very shortly I shall signal you to stop as in an emergency, as though a child had run off the pavement. The signal will be like this (the examiner will be at the edge of the road and raise his or her right arm). When I give this signal, stop immediately and under full control wherever you are. The sign will not be given if danger to other traffic is likely to arise.' The examiner will direct you on the route you should ride, which is usually a left-hand circuit that will take you round the block and back to where the examiner will be waiting. You will be asked if you understand what has been explained. If you say yes, the examiner will say, 'move off when you're ready please.' Should you have any doubt about where you have to ride, ask the examiner to repeat the instruction. It should be borne in mind that this exercise is meant to simulate a real emergency, and so you will have to prove to the examiner that you can meet the requirements needed in this situation. This is the only time throughout the test that you will not be accompanied while riding, and you *do not* take rear observation before stopping.

If you understand the instructions given, get ready to move off when it is safe to do so. Take effective rear observation and look well ahead, then move away safely and under control. Proceed on the route that has been explained to you. As you approach the examiner, look for the signal to stop. If it is not given, this is because it is not safe to do the exercise due to traffic following you at the time. Therefore, continue on the same route that will take you round the block again. As you approach the examiner and the signal for you to stop is given, apply the front and then the back brake. Remember the rules of braking!

The object of this exercise is to stop in the shortest possible distance, promptly and under control, by making proper use of the brakes. Brake pressure should vary according to the road surface. If either wheel should start to lock (causing you to skid), release the brakes and immediately reapply them with less pressure in the same sequence as before. The clutch should remain engaged until it is necessary to disengage it to prevent the engine from stalling. At the same time, the

reduction of engine speed will help to slow the machine down. As soon as the machine comes to a halt, select neutral gear and stop the engine.

The examiner has given instructions for the emergency stop exercise. You will then be asked to 'ride on when you're ready'. The rider is taking effective rear observation before moving off on to the route that has been described to him.

As you approach the examiner, he or she will give the signal to STOP. As soon as you see the signal, apply the brakes, bearing in mind the condition of the road surface. Remember the rules of braking. The rider has applied the brakes and is about to stop. Note the rider's left foot is about to touch the road while the rear brake is still being applied.

As soon as you see the signal to stop, you should apply the brakes immediately. Do not lock (skid) either wheel or stall the engine. If you do, a (control) fault will be recorded.

When you have brought the machine to rest, select neutral gear and stop the engine. The examiner will then ask you to move nearer to the kerb, so that the instructions for the next exercise, which is the 'U' turn, can be explained to you.

The 'U' turn

You will be asked to turn the machine round to face the opposite way by doing a 'U' turn within the kerbs.

The three points that you should be able to demonstrate to the examiner in this exercise are good balance, machine control, and due regard for other road users while turning in the road.

The examiner has given the rider the instructions for this exercise. The rider is ready to move off. All round observation has been taken and the rider is waiting for an oncoming vehicle to pass. When the road is clear of traffic and no pedestrians are likely to cross, the rider will start the exercise.

The rider has moved away safely and is maintaining good machine control and balance. The examiner will record any fault(s) made by the rider. When the rider has reached the other side of the road, rear observation should be taken before stopping parallel with the kerb, as requested by the examiner.

The rider will now have to get the machine back across the road to where the examiner is standing. This can be achieved either by pushing or riding the machine across the road. This is not part of the test, but the objective should still be achieved while having due regard for other road users.

During the 'U' turn, if a rider stalls the engine, uses the throttle excessively, puts a foot down or rides with a foot or feet continuously on the ground to help balance, these faults will be recorded by the examiner.

The slow ride

Another requirement of the motorcycle test is the slow ride. The examiner will ask you to pull up on the left. When you have done so, the examiner will ask you to ride forward at walking pace, as if in slow-moving traffic, and move off when you are ready. The distance you should ride during this exercise is about 25 metres.

The faults that can be committed by a rider during the slow ride are: poor machine control, ie excessive use of the throttle, and poor balance, ie putting one or two feet on the road to maintain balance.

This rider is wobbling, and a foot is being put down to steady his balance. The machine should be ridden smoothly and not in jerky movements. Imagine yourself in the middle of heavy, slow-moving traffic.

Effective rear observation

Regardless of whether you have mirrors fitted to your machine or not, you should always look over your shoulder and take effective rear observation before signalling, changing direction, slowing down or stopping. You must be aware of the traffic situation behind you and react appropriately to the situation.

Signalling

By looking well ahead, the rider can see a stationary vehicle that must be passed. The rider is taking effective rear observation before a signal of his intention to change course is given.

Changing direction

THE LIFESAVER LOOK

The rider is about to turn right. The System of Motorcycle Control (as shown on pages 113–36) has been implemented apart from the final rear observation before changing direction. The rider is now taking final effective rear observation before changing direction. A vehicle can be seen in an overtaking position and its estimated speed is 40 mph. Reacting to what he can see, the rider decides to proceed on a straight course, thus cancelling his intention to turn right.

The driver of the car is about to overtake the rider at the wrong time and place (a junction). This inconsiderate and dangerous attitude has been the cause of numerous serious and fatal accidents. In this situation, the rider prevented an accident occurring due to effective rear observation and taking the appropriate action.

It can be seen from this example why the last rear observation before changing direction is called the 'lifesaver'.

When turning left, the last rear observation ('lifesaver') is taken by looking over the left shoulder, just before reaching the corner.

This rider did not take effective rear observation before changing direction and, therefore, was not aware of the following vehicle. A potentially dangerous fault has been committed and consequently, the following vehicle has been forced to brake hard.

Slowing down or stopping

The intention of the rider is to follow the road ahead at the crossroads. A give way sign can be seen and, therefore, speed will have to be reduced. Effective rear observation is being taken before slowing down or stopping, so that the rider can check the position of any following traffic.

Poor observation

This rider did not take effective rear observation before moving away. Therefore, he has created a potentially dangerous situation for another road user and for himself.

Rear observation at the wrong time and place

A rider should take effective rear observation at the right time and place, if practicably possible. The car and motorcycle are both travelling at 30 mph but the motorcyclist is following the car too closely. If the rider decides to take rear observation at the same time as the driver of the car decides to stop, a serious or fatal accident could occur because the rider took rear observation at the wrong time and place and when it was not safe to do so.

Give signals where necessary, correctly and in good time

A signal given by a motorcyclist whether it is an arm, direction indicator or stop lamp signal, is a means by which a rider warns other road users of his or her intention. Signals are the language of the road and are the only visible way in which riders can inform other road users and pedestrians of their intention and presence.

To be of any use, signals must be given clearly, as illustrated in *The Highway Code*, and at the right time and place. A signal gives a warning, *not* an instruction, and gives no right of way whatsoever to carry out an intended action. Too many serious accidents are caused by drivers and motorcyclists who do not signal their intention to carry out a manoeuvre, or do not signal correctly or in good time.

The rider here has not signalled his intention to turn right, and at the same time, the driver of the car decides to overtake him. A serious or fatal accident could be a few seconds away. You must *always* signal to let other road users know what you intend to do.

Signal omitted
This rider has failed to signal his intention to turn right, thus creating a
potentially dangerous situation for himself and other road users.

Late signal
The rider is about to change course in order to pass a stationary vehicle. A signal is about to be given but will be too late to be of any use to following traffic.

Signalling incorrectly

The intention of this rider is to turn left at the cross roads. However, he has signalled too early because he is in the wrong position in the road, due to a parked vehicle ahead. A change of course to the right will have to be made but because the incorrect signal is being given, a potentially dangerous situation could arise if traffic is following.

The intention of this rider is to turn right at a
'T' junction. His road position is correct but
the signal being shown by the direction
indicator is indicating the intention to turn
left. Again, a dangerous situation could arise
due to incorrect signalling.

Traffic signs; road markings; signals given by traffic controllers.

Prompt and appropriate action should be taken when any of these are encountered.

Traffic signs
A rider intending to turn left at the next junction can see road works in the road that is about to be joined. In this situation, it must be remembered that any traffic emerging from the left should be given the right of way.

Therefore, effective observation to the left must be taken in good time, in order to assess the situation before reaching the hazard.

You *must* comply with a STOP sign, even if the road to be joined is seen to be clear.

If you take your test in a rural area, the test route may include a level crossing. Like any other crossing that is controlled by traffic signals, it should be approached with caution. This will give you time to comply with the traffic signal shown at the time of your approach.

Road markings

At this junction, the road markings direct you to turn right nearside to nearside. Therefore, you should comply strictly with the markings shown. All road markings should be closely observed and correctly acted upon.

Traffic controllers
You must comply with any signal given by a police officer.

Exercise proper care in the use of speed

Proper care must always be exercised in the use of speed and this will
be impressed upon you from the very beginning of your training.

When forward vision is obscured, you must reduce speed so that you
are able to stop in the distance you can see to be clear.

During the test, you will be expected to ride at a safe speed according to the prevailing road and traffic conditions. You should not ride slowly, holding up the following traffic, when the road and traffic conditions allow you to ride faster.

Some test routes have roads that have a speed limit in excess of 30 mph. Because this road is very clear, straight and flat, the rider is travelling at the maximum allowed speed of 40 mph.

Act properly at road junctions
Take effective observation before emerging

When approaching a junction, whatever its type or layout, a complete assessment of the situation must be made before a decision to proceed is taken. If traffic can be seen approaching, or the view to either side is obscured, then you should stop at the junction.

As the rider approaches this T-junction, the view to either side is obscured by trees. Therefore, the rider stops at the junction to gain a clear view.

To gain a better view, which is vital in this situation, the rider has moved forward to increase his vision, at the same time watching out for any traffic that could be approaching. When a clear view to either side is obtained, the decision to proceed can be made.

If traffic can be seen approaching, let it pass, then look right, left and right again. If all is clear, take rear observation and proceed, providing it is still safe to do so.

This rider did not take effective observation on the approach to and at the junction. Consequently the rider still decided to proceed, and in doing so, has emerged into the path of an approaching vehicle. The action taken by this rider has been, and still is, the cause of many serious and fatal accidents.

Regulate speed correctly on approach

There have been numerous accidents at uncontrolled junctions caused by excessive speed on approach. You should always approach a junction at a speed at which you can easily stop, as and when you have to.

Position the vehicle correctly before turning right.

This rider has positioned himself too far to the left for turning right. In doing so, he is creating an obstruction for any following traffic.

This rider intends to turn right at the junction ahead. Because he has positioned himself incorrectly, he has created a dangerous situation for himself.

This rider is riding on the hazard line, which is not the correct position for turning right, and again, is not safe.

This rider has been requested to turn right at the end of the road, but seems confused as to where he should be on the road. This is obviously unsafe. Make sure you know exactly where to position yourself on the road when turning either left or right.

Position the vehicle correctly before turning left

This rider has positioned himself too far to the right for turning left. Consequently, he is creating an obstacle for any following traffic.

This rider has tried to take a short cut by cutting a right-hand corner while turning right. In doing so, he has created a situation dangerous for another road user, who has had to brake hard to prevent an accident. Do *not* cut right-hand corners while turning right.

The System of Motorcycle Control at junctions

The System of Motorcycle Control is a system or drill, each feature of which is considered in sequence on the approach to any hazard. It is the basis upon which the techniques of good motorcycling are built.

The System of Motorcycle Control was devised in 1937. It creates a simple and repetitive method of riding which ensures that the rider omits no detail and leaves nothing to chance. When perfected, it gives that one vital ingredient that is essential to safe motorcycling – *time to react*. During your training, you will be taught the System. You should always remember that if you omit one feature of the system when it should have been used, you leave something to chance, and that one omission could prove fatal.

Turning left at a cross roads

Step 1 – Rear observation

The examiner has given the instruction 'take the next road on the left please'. Rear observation is taken so that the presence and position of any following traffic is known.

The ideal course is that of normal road position, with little or no deviation, unless circumstances dictate that a parked vehicle or other obstruction has to be passed. Then, a change of course will have to be made.

Step 2 and 3 – Signal, speed and gear

The left-hand direction indicator is used and confirmed by an 'I intend to turn left' arm signal.

When the arm signal has been given, the rider should reduce speed by proper use of the brakes, or deceleration where this is sufficient. A gear should then be selected that is appropriate to the road speed and that will respond to the throttle.

Step 4 – Rear observation

Rear observation is taken again to check the movement and position of any following traffic.

Step 5 – Signal

Although a direction indicator signal has been in use since step 2, an arm signal should be considered again (if practicable) to emphasise and confirm the intention to turn left.

Step 6 – Rear observation ('lifesaver')

Rear observation is taken by looking over the left shoulder. In doing so, the rider will be fully aware of any following traffic.

While the rider is following the kerb line to the 'give way' lines, all-round effective observation is taken.

While effective observation is being taken, traffic can be seen approaching. The rider has, therefore, made the correct decision to stop.

Step 7 - Acceleration
When it is safe to do so, the rider completes the left turn and accelerates away from the junction.

Straight ahead at a crossroads

Step 1 - Rear observation and course

Rear observation is taken so that the position and speed of any following traffic is known. The layout of the junction is the deciding factor in changing course, as one crossroad can vary from another, and should never be assumed to be standard in layout.

Step 2 - Signal and speed

A slowing down signal is considered and should be used if there is any following traffic. As there isn't, and there are no pedestrians ahead, a slowing down signal at this time and place is not justified. Speed is reduced by proper use of the brakes.

Step 3 - Gear and rear observation
When speed has been reduced, the appropriate gear should be selected, so that the rider can approach the junction at the correct speed. Rear observation is taken again and an 'I intend to slow down' arm signal is considered.

Step 4 - Course and observation
The rider has adopted the correct course for this particular junction. Effective observation is being taken to the right, left and right again, before the decision is made to continue.

As the rider approaches this junction, a vehicle can be seen approaching from the right. The rider has no option but to stop at the 'give way' lines.

While waiting for the vehicle to pass, another one can be seen in the distance.

Step 5 – Rear observation

Because of the layout of the junction, the rider has adopted the correct position on the road but, in doing so, has put himself in a vulnerable position. Therefore, when the road is clear to either side of him, rear observation is taken over the right shoulder.

Rear observation is then taken over the left shoulder, and to each side again. If all is clear, and the road ahead is seen to be clear, the decision is made to move forward.

The rider accelerates away from the 'give way' lines, followed by the examiner.

Turning right at a T-junction

Step 1 – Rear observation

The examiner has given the candidate the instruction, 'at the end of the road, please turn right'. From a normal riding position on the nearside, it will be necessary to move out to just left of the centre of the road. This should be done in good time and rear observation must be taken beforehand by looking over the right shoulder, to see what is behind.

Step 2 – Signal

A right-hand direction indicator signal is used, and confirmed by an 'I intend to move out to the right' arm signal.

Step 3 – Observation

Rear observation is taken again to check the movement and position of any following traffic, making sure it is safe to change course to just left of the centre of the road. You must remember that the situation to the rear of the rider could have changed since step 1. It should never be assumed that the situation behind is still clear of following traffic. Consequently, rear observation must be taken again.

Step 4 – Manoeuvre and course

When the rider has ensured that it is safe to do so, a change of course is made to just left of the centre of the road. The absence of centre line road markings is no excuse for positioning the machine incorrectly.

When the manoeuvre has been completed, rear observation is taken again to check the position of any following traffic. The rider is on the ideal course for a right turn.

Step 5 – Signal

Although a direction indicator signal has been in use since step 2, an arm signal should also be given (if practicable) to emphasise and confirm the intention to turn right.

Step 6 – Speed and look

The rider is aware of the presence of any following traffic. Road speed is reduced by braking or deceleration, if sufficient.

The rider is taking effective observation by looking right, left and right again before reaching the junction. The observant rider will take full advantage of open spaces and gaps in hedges or fences (as the rider is doing here), to get that valuable but brief view of the road into which he is going to turn. The rider should always remember that the speed on approach to a junction is related directly to the view available to the right and left. The more restricted the view, the slower the approach, thus allowing time and distance to stop at the junction should you need to.

Step 7 – Rear observation ('lifesaver')

A last look over the right shoulder is essential to make sure that any following traffic has responded to the signals given, and that it is safe to start turning right.

When it is safe to do so the rider completes the right turn without cutting the corner. Rear observation should be taken when the manoeuvre has been completed. The examiner can be seen following the candidate, observing all his actions.

*The System of Motorcycle
Control at roundabouts*

Turning right at a roundabout

Step 1 – Rear observation

The examiner has given the candidate the instruction 'at the roundabout, take the road leading off to the right, please'. Rear observation is taken by looking over the right shoulder. In doing this, the rider will be aware of the movement and position of any following traffic.

Step 2 – Signal

A right-hand direction indicator signal is used and confirmed by an 'I intend to move out to the right' arm signal. Always remember that an arm or indicator signal does not give the rider right of way. It is a signal of *intention*.

Step 3 – Rear observation
Rear observation is taken again to check the movement and position of following traffic, making sure it is safe to change course for a right turn. This should be done in good time.

Step 4 – Manoeuvre and course
When it is safe to do so, a change of course has to be made to just left of the centre of the road.

The rider is now in the correct position on the road.

Step 5 – Rear observation
Rear observation is taken again to check the movement and position of following traffic.

Step 6 – Signal
Although a direction indicator signal is being used, an arm signal should also be given (if practicable) as confirmation of the signal being used, thus making your intention absolutely clear to other road users.

Step 7 – Speed and look

At this point, the rider should reduce road speed by proper use of the brakes, or deceleration, if sufficient.

While reducing speed, observation across and to the right of the roundabout should be taken, thereby giving way to any traffic approaching, if necessary. If no traffic can be seen, no further braking should be necessary.

Step 8 – Rear observation ('lifesaver')

A last look over the left shoulder is essential to make sure that following traffic has responded to the signals given and that it is safe to start turning.

Step 9 – Position

When it is safe to do so, move on to the offside position on the roundabout, and keep to that position until step 11.

Step 10 – Rear observation ('lifesaver') and signal

The next exit on the left is to be taken, and so rear observation should be taken by looking over the left shoulder ('lifesaver') and a left direction indicator signal given. Remember that any danger will be on the immediate left and to the rear of the rider.

Step 11 – Course and rear observation ('lifesaver')

In order to take the next exit on the left, the recommended course as shown in *The Highway Code* should be used and rear observation ('lifesaver') over the left shoulder must be taken before a change of course is made.

Following the road ahead at a roundabout

Step 1 – Rear observation

The examiner has given the instruction, 'at the roundabout, follow the road ahead, please'. Rear observation is taken to check the presence and position of any following traffic.

Step 2 – Speed and look

Road speed should be reduced by deceleration or proper use of the brakes. At the same time, observation across and to the right of the roundabout is taken, and what can or cannot be seen determines how much you reduce your speed. This will give the rider adequate time and distance to give way or stop for approaching traffic if there is any.

Step 3 – Rear observation ('lifesaver')

A last look over the left shoulder is essential, so that the rider is aware of any potential danger on the near side and to the immediate rear.

As the rider joins the roundabout, observation is taken to the left to check any approaching traffic from the left.

Step 4 – Rear observation ('lifesaver') and signal
Rear observation to the left is taken so that the presence of any potential danger is observed. A left-hand direction signal is now used.

Step 5 – Observation ('lifesaver')
Rear observation to the nearside is taken again before changing course to leave the roundabout. This 'lifesaver' look assures the rider of the presence of any potential danger before he changes course.

Turning left at a roundabout

Step 1 - Rear observation

The examiner has given the candidate the instruction, 'At the roundabout, take the next road on the left, please'. Rear observation is taken by looking over the right shoulder, enabling the rider to check the position of any following traffic.

Step 2 - Signal

A left-hand direction indicator signal is used and confirmed by an 'I intend to turn left' arm signal. The confirmation arm signal is of the utmost importance for obvious reasons, especially when the sun is behind the rider. The brightness of sunlight could obscure the light given by the indicator signal, making the rider's intention to turn left unknown to following road users.

Step 3 – Rear observation

Rear observation is taken again to check the position of any following traffic. If there is no obstruction ahead, no deviation in course should be necessary. However, speed must be reduced, either by deceleration or by using the brakes.

Step 4 – Signal

Although a left-hand direction indicator signal is being used, another 'I intend to turn left' arm signal should be used. This is done to emphasise and confirm your intention to turn left, as the traffic situation behind could have changed since giving the first arm signal.

Step 5 - Speed and look

At this point, the rider should reduce road speed by proper use of the brakes, except where deceleration is sufficient.

While reducing speed, observation across and to the right of the roundabout should be taken, so that you are able to give way to any traffic approaching. If no traffic can be seen, no further braking should be necessary.

Step 6 - Rear observation ('lifesaver')

The last look is over the left shoulder. This is essential to make sure that following traffic has responded to the signals given, and no other road user has crept up on your nearside. A final look to the right should be taken as the situation could have changed since step 5.

Step 7 – Manoeuvre and acceleration

Provided it is safe to do so, the rider starts the manoeuvre to join the road on the left, while at the same time looking well ahead. Acceleration is being applied to leave the turn, although the condition of the road surface on and away from the turn must be considered when increasing speed.

Overtaking

Thoughtless overtaking at the wrong time and place has been the cause of many fatal road accidents. During a journey, a motorcyclist will pass many stationary and moving vehicles; those travelling in the same direction as himself, he is said to 'overtake'. To do this safely, the System of Motorcycle Control must be applied. Although the System is the same as that for fixed hazards, it is more complex because during the process of overtaking, a number of subsidiary hazards may arise and have to be dealt with in conjunction with the primary hazard.

The rider here has made the decision to overtake. Rear observation has been taken and a signal of intent given by using a right-hand direction indicator signal. Rear observation is taken again before a change of course is made to the correct overtaking position. A good margin of safety has been allowed between the rider and the vehicle being overtaken. The time, place and distance required to accomplish this manoeuvre is considered before any decision to overtake is made. If there is any doubt, the rider would not have started the manoeuvre.

Overtaking faults

This rider is too close to the vehicle that he is overtaking and has not allowed a margin for safety. Should the driver not see the motorcyclist and suddenly steer to the right to avoid a pothole, for instance, a serious accident could occur.

Always allow a good margin of safety while overtaking. If in any doubt, do not start the manoeuvre.

This rider should have allowed a greater distance from the vehicle being overtaken before returning to the left. By cutting in here, he has created a dangerous situation for himself and the car driver.

Always make sure you are well clear of the vehicle that you have overtaken by taking effective rear observation before moving back to the normal riding position on the left-hand side of the road.

This rider has made a thoughtless overtaking manoeuvre, and consequently, has become 'the meat in the sandwich'. This expression came about many years ago after a fatal accident in which a motorcyclist was crushed between two vehicles while overtaking. This rider should have held back until the approaching vehicle had passed, and then, when safe, he could have started the manoeuvre.

Meet other vehicles safely

This rider has forced his way through a gap between two vehicles that have not been parked very considerately. This has forced an oncoming driver to take evasive action. If the driver had had the same attitude as the rider, a serious or fatal accident could have occurred.

A good rider would have formulated a safe riding plan on the approach to the hazard. Rear observation would have been taken, speed reduced and, if necessary, the machine would be brought to a rest, allowing the driver to dictate the situation. Prudence is a great virtue. When in doubt, apply it.

Cross the path of other vehicles safely

This rider is in the correct position on the road before turning right. An opposing vehicle is approaching and so the decision to wait has been made until it is safe to turn. This is in compliance with *The Highway Code*.

This rider has decided to turn right when it is not safe to do so, because of the oncoming vehicle. The dangerous and irresponsible action taken by the rider has forced another road user to take evasive action in braking hard to avoid colliding with the rider. Misjudgement of speed and distance, or a careless attitude on the part of the rider, has been the cause of many serious and fatal accidents while turning right.

Road position

Always assume the correct road position when riding.

   A vehicle can be seen here on the left, waiting to emerge. The rider has taken rear observation by looking over his right shoulder and should be asking himself 'has the driver of the car seen me? Did he look right? If so, did the lamppost obscure his view? If it did, will he take it for granted that the road to either side is clear and so start to emerge? The rider should anticipate the car moving out and across his path.

   The motorcyclist, however, is riding in the correct position on the road and, therefore, should be seen by the driver of the car.

System for passing parked vehicles

Having seen the hazard ahead, the rider must formulate a safe riding plan to be able to pass the hazard with maximum safety to himself and to that of any other road user(s). The riding plan adopted should leave nothing to chance, and so it should always be borne in mind that the situation could change before the hazard is passed.

Step 1 – Rear observation

Before changing course to pass the hazard, the rider must make sure it is safe to do so. The rider is taking good effective rear observation and checking the position and speed of any following traffic.

Step 2 – Signal

A signal of intent to move out to the right is given by direction indicator and is reinforced by an 'I intend to move out' arm signal. Adequate time is allowed to change course well before reaching the hazard.

Step 3 – Rear observation

Rear observation is taken again, as the position and speed of any following traffic could have changed since rear observation was first taken. If safe to do so, a change in course is now made so that the hazard can be passed with a good margin of safety.

Step 4 – Course

The rider is on an ideal course for passing the hazard. The driver can be seen opening the door and starting to get out of the vehicle, obviously before making sure it is safe to do so. However, the rider has not been put in a dangerous situation as adequate clearance has been allowed. The potential danger was considered in the riding plan and, therefore, it was avoided. The rider has now cancelled the direction indicator signal, so as not to confuse any other road user by over-use of signals.

Step 5 – Rear observation

When the hazard has been passed, rear observation by looking over the left shoulder should be taken before changing course to the nearside, providing it is safe to do so.

Step 6 – Course
The rider is now returning to the normal riding position on the road.

This rider is about to pass a stationary vehicle which looks as if it is going to move off, regardless of the presence of the passing motorcyclist. The rider is taking no chances as to whether the driver has seen him or not. Therefore, the rider has applied the brakes and is preparing to stop. In doing so, he has taken appropriate action in preventing an accident. It only takes one irresponsible driver to act thoughtlessly to cause a serious or fatal accident.

A driver who has adjusted the off-side door mirror correctly, should have a good view along the off-side of the vehicle. You must always bear in mind that some motorists move off or manoeuvre regardless of what can be seen in the mirror(s), and there are those who do not use the mirror(s) at all. Therefore, a rider should, if practicably possible, allow an adequate margin of safety when passing a stationary vehicle(s).

To all intents and purposes, a driver can look in the off-side door mirror, and thinking it is safe to move off, will do so. As a result, he or she could collide with a passing motorcyclist that was not seen in the blind spot of the mirror.

A driver should always look over his or her shoulder to check the blind area that cannot be seen in the mirror(s). Some drivers are irresponsible and fail to do this. Therefore, motorcyclists should always pass a vehicle with extreme caution.

Pedestrian crossings

When approaching a zebra crossing, look out for pedestrians waiting to cross (particularly children, the elderly, the disabled and people with prams) and be ready to slow down or stop to let them cross.

The rider is giving an 'I intend to slow down or stop' arm signal. In doing so, the pedestrian(s) and other traffic are aware of the rider's intention.

This rider has no riding plan. The pedestrian crossing is of no concern to him.

An offence has been committed and a dangerous situation has arisen. The rider has not complied with *The Highway Code*.

Select a safe position for normal stops

During the test, you will be asked on a number of occasions to pull up on the left at a convenient place. The purpose of stopping on the left is so that the examiner can see if you can bring the machine to rest properly, and at a safe place, and then to see if you can move away safely and under control.

This rider was requested to pull up on the left, and in doing so, has *not* complied with *The Highway Code*. He is unaware of the obstruction he has created for another road user who cannot now leave a private driveway. Always try to comply with *The Highway Code* when and where you stop.

Show awareness and anticipation of the actions of pedestrians, cyclists and car drivers

Pedestrians

A rider should always adopt a safe riding plan. This can only be achieved by thinking and looking well ahead. In doing so, he or she should be aware of and anticipate what other road users are going to do, thus giving him or herself time to take the appropriate action.

This rider did not look well ahead, and therefore, has not anticipated the action being taken by the careless pedestrian, who is more concerned with the newspaper than with the Green Cross Code! The rider will have to reduce speed suddenly, which could cause an accident if traffic is following.

The movement of pedestrians can be unpredictable, and therefore, speed should be reduced when there are a lot of pedestrians about. This allows you plenty of time and distance to stop.

These pedestrians have no regard for the Green Cross Code or their own safety.

Cyclists

Cyclists can be seen here using the cycle path. It should not be taken for granted that they will stay on their present course. A wide margin of safety should, therefore, be allowed when passing them.

Car drivers

The car in front has just reversed onto a main road. The front wheels are turned to the left, and so it looks as if the driver is about to move off. Acting on what can be seen, the rider should take rear observation and reduce speed, thereby leaving nothing to chance. The rider should let the driver move off, so avoiding any potential danger.

Pass or fail

When you arrive back at the test centre, the machine should be parked close to the kerb, and the appropriate stand used. The machine should be properly secured and the petrol tap in the off position, before you leave the machine unattended.

Having removed your helmet and radio equipment, the examiner will then ask you some questions on *The Highway Code* and other motoring matters. Remember that this is still part of the test and that you will fail if you do not answer the questions correctly.

The examiner will then tell you whether or not you have passed your test. If you have failed, the examiner will inform you on which elements of the test you committed faults and, consequently, which areas of your riding you need to practise and improve. If you have passed (congratulations!), the examiner will fill out a certificate which you must sign to prove that you have passed. You must send this, together with your provisional licence and the appropriate form completed (obtainable from the Post Office), to DVLA (formerly DVLC), Swansea so that your licence can be updated to a full one for the group you are applying for.

Here is a specimen of a full European Communities driving licence (front) which you will receive, having passed your test and made an application to the DVLA.

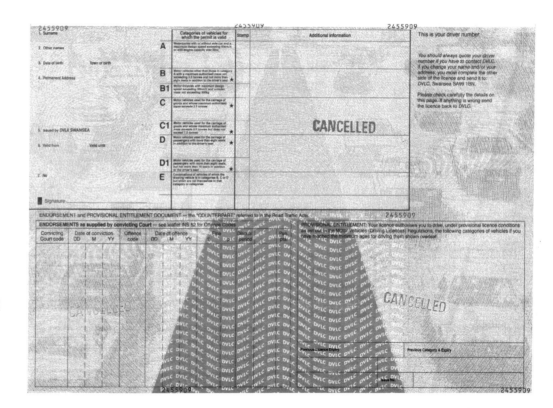

A specimen of a full European Communities driving licence* (back).

*This licence is under Crown Copyright and is reproduced with the kind permission of the Controller of Her Majesty's Stationery Office.

Conclusion

Much has been written and illustrated in this book that explains how to develop your motorcycle riding skills. There are many thousands of qualified motorcyclists riding today, who have achieved that status with the help and advice given in the first edition of *The Castrol Motorcycle Manual*, published in 1985.

You must remember that the information given in this book is not only to help you pass the Compulsory Basic Training (CBT) course, thereby receiving validation of your provisional driving licence. Nor is this book merely to help you obtain a full category 'A' driving licence when you pass the road test, carried out from a Driving Standards Agency Driving Test Centre. The test is just the start of your driving career. You should not assume that if you pass, you are a good rider with nothing more to learn, which is the belief of many. Developing the correct attitude and riding with responsibility and consideration for other road users are vital aspects of good motorcycling. This can only be achieved by applying all that you have learned during training every time you ride your machine. It has often been said that good riders are born and not made, but to become a good rider, training is an essential ingredient. By demonstrating the numerous aspects of the CBT and the motorcycle test in this book, I hope that I have highlighted some of the fundamental principles of safe and skilled motorcyling.

Good riding!

Gordon Cole
Road Safety Officer
Harrow Driving Centre
Alexandra Avenue
South Harrow
Middlesex
HA2 9DA
Tel: 081-422 5883

Other driving titles by Gordon Cole include:

DRIVE AND SURVIVE *also published by Kogan Page*

and

SAFER MOTORWAY DRIVING
ADVANCED DRIVING
PASS THE DRIVING TEST
TAKE YOUR CAR ABROAD *all published by Ian Allan Ltd*

All available from good bookshops